Marine Life For Young Readers

Butterflies of the Sea

Contents

Text by Stanley L. Swartz
Photography by Robert Yin

DOMINIE PRESS
Pearson Learning Group

About Sea Slugs

Sea slugs are very colorful.
They are also graceful swimmers.
Sometimes they are called the
butterflies of the sea.

◀ Bullock's slug

4

How They Swim

Sea slugs are slow swimmers. Their **flaps** help them swim. They live in **salt water**.

◀ Yellow-skirted slug

Their Mollusk Family

Sea slugs are part of the **mollusk** family. Clams are in this family and have a shell. Sea slugs are soft and have no shell.

◄ Willan's slug

Small Wonders

Sea slugs lay **thousands** of eggs.
Most sea slugs are small. They range
in size from two to twelve inches.

◀ Bullock's slug

Where They Live

Sea slugs live on **coral reefs**.
Their favorite food is sponges.
They also eat small animals.

◀ Checkered Sidegill slug

How They Hide

Some sea slugs are poisonous. Their spots warn other animals. The spots also help **camouflage** the sea slug so that it can hide from enemies.

◄ Tryon's slug

How They Feel

They have two **tentacles** on their head. They use the tentacles to feel. These tentacles can **retract**.

◀ Black-striped Yellow slug

How They Breathe

Their gills look like **feathers**.

Gills are used for breathing.

The gills form a circle on their back.

◄ Willan's slug

18

Other sea slugs are **smooth**.
You cannot see their gills.
They breathe through their skin.

◀ Red-ringed Sidegill slug

The Spanish Dancer

The Spanish Dancer is bright red. Its name comes from its shape and color. It looks like the **fringe** of a dress when it swims.

◀ Spanish Dancer

Butterflies of the Sea

There are many different kinds of sea slugs. Their graceful swimming and beautiful colors truly make them the butterflies of the sea.

◄ Yellow Polka-dotted slug

Glossary

butterflies: Flying insects, usually colorful

camouflage: To cover or disguise; to hide something

coral reefs: Hard shelves of coral

feathers: The long, soft covering of a bird

flaps: Folds of skin that move

fringe: An edge or border

mollusk: A family of soft sea animals

retract: To pull in

salt water: Water in the ocean that has a large amount of salt

smooth: Free from bumps; not rough

tentacles: Long body parts used to feel

thousands: 10 x 100 = 1,000

Index